The Netherlands Cookbook

*To my american relatives
and many english friends
and to all Dutch people who emigrated to
various parts of the world.*

Heleen A. M. Halverhout

THE NETHERLANDS
COOKBOOK

AMSTERDAM/DE DRIEHOEK

ISBN 90 6030 002 5

Dear friends of our Dutch food.

In this little book you will find some of our traditional dishes, which you probably liked when dining out or at the home of Dutch friends.

We "Hollanders" as we are mostly called in the States (in England they call us "the Dutch") are great lovers of nice food. And we like to prepare these tasty dishes from the best ingredients. We like to eat them at home in the company of our family, seated at a well-set table, — covered in the Dutch way with a tablecloth of white or colored linen —, under a big lamp fixed in the middle of the ceiling of our diningroom.

Our traditional dishes are mostly based on rather nourishing ingredients, but as you probably know we take only one hot meal a day. The first and the second meal are sandwich-meals. In my recipes I give the amount 4 Dutch persons would eat. Maybe the amount you would use would be different; that is up to you to decide. There are of course exceptions, because certain dishes or certain baked goods must be made as given in the recipe and I have given you recipes of dishes which are within the scope of the average housewife and made of ingredients you can get at home.

May I give you a suggestion when to make one or more of the following recipes?

When you ask your friends to a "do" after coming back from your trip to Europe, or

at a church-social, in aid of some good purpose, or

when entertaining "Hollanders". They will be delighted with your charming idea, or

at so many other occasions, as you will know best.

It has been a very great pleasure to write this little book for you. It is always so nice to know that visitors to my country are interested in our "Dutch Fare". I wish you "good cooking" and much fun preparing these typical dishes of the Netherlands.

And to my countrymen and women: I hope you will enjoy these typical Dutch dishes, maybe you will adjust them to your own liking: "As mother used to make it".

Yours sincerely

HELEEN A. M. HALVERHOUT.

Our food habits.

The people in the Netherlands have other "food habits" than other people on the continent, in the United Kingdom or the United States of America. This sounds probably a bit funny for such a small country. But it is a fact and you know the saying: Do in Rome as the Romans do. Freely translated: When in Holland, eat as we do. May I give you a short description of the way we serve our meals?

For breakfast we have bread and butter, or open sandwiches with jam, cheese, "ontbijtkoek" (see recipe page 96). We drink tea with it, or milk, maybe buttermilk. Sometimes we have a boiled egg and children may have a plateful of "pap".

At 11 o'clock ("elevenses") we drink one or more cups of coffee with cream

or milk. And treat ourselves to a piece of (buttered) "koek" or some "boterkoek" (see recipe page 88) or cake, for extra festive occasions.

At lunchtime   we have another bread and butter meal. Maybe some rolls are

put on the table (krentenbroodjes, cadetjes, halve maantjes = croissants) and Dutch rusks topped with cheese or jam.

With it we have some meat: liver sausage or ham; maybe a fried egg or two or an omelette. When guests arrive we make a special hot dish: croquettes or macaroni cheese, or ham and cheese savory (see recipe page 31).

Fruits finish off the meal with which we drink coffee, milk, buttermilk or cocoa.

At 4 o'clock it is teatime. A cup of tea and a biscuit is quite usual.

For special occasions we produce fancy cakes, cookies or chocolates.

At 5 o'clock the Dutch drink a "Borrel" (Dutch gin), see page 104 for the famous "Bitterballen".

At 6 o'clock it is dinner time. Our first hot meal *. Mainly consisting of:

> a hot entrée (soup)
> or a cold entrée,
> meat or fish with vegetables and potatoes,
> sometimes a sweet or fruit to finish.

Only on special occasions wine or beer is served.
Coffee may be served after the meal, but is mostly not taken at the dining table.

* Never expect fruit juice or Coca Cola *with* your meal.

8 o'clock tea again with biscuits. And maybe people prefer coffee.

Cookies, cake or a more elaborate baked sweet is offered, when we have company (visitors).

Some people like to drink beer or wine or Dutch gin (jenever) maybe a liqueur or whisky later on.

You see . . . it is different. But you will certainly enjoy it when you are offered these things in the home of a Dutch family.

Mind you, I have nothing against hotels but they do not serve you "real Dutch meals", as you would be served in a typical Dutch home.

*) In some parts of the Netherlands the hot meal is served at midday and a bread and butter meal in the evening.

12

Note.

In the recipes you will find either the word Holland or Dutch (officially "the Netherlands"). In America one might mix Dutch = Pensylvanian Dutch, originally German people coming to America speaking Deutsch (German). In England the word Dutch is connected with their overseas neighbours in Holland.  Therefore the same words have not always the same meaning in England or America. Also "cooking ingredients" have not the same meaning.

If in England another word is used, it is put in parentheses e.g. molasses (treacle).

American cookery terms.	English cookery terms.
confectioner's sugar	icing sugar.
farina	semolina.
sifted	sieved.
candied cherries	glacé cherries.
preserve	jam.
pudding mold	blanc mange mould.
self-rising flour	self-raising flour.
pancover	saucepan lid.
chili	hot red pepper. Spanish pepper.
casserole	oven-proof dish.
platter	serving dish.
pre-cooked	quick boiling.
midmorning "coffee break"	"elevenses".
ground	minced.

14

Temperatures given in both degrees Fahrenheit and degrees Celcius (centigrade) because of the beginning of the changeover to centigrade setting in Great Britain by 1970.

Hints for using this book. Oven temperatures.

American gas and electric oven temperatures are given in degrees Fahrenheit.

temperature	term
250° F—275° F	very slow oven
300° F—325° F	slow oven
350° F—375° F	moderate oven
400° F—425° F	hot oven
450° F—475° F	very hot oven
500° F—525° F	extremely hot oven

English gas and electric oven temperatures compared.

gas oven marks	approximate temp. in centre of gas oven	electric oven settings	term
¼	240° F (115° C)	200° F (95° C)	cool oven
½	265° F (130° C)	225° F (110° C)	cool oven
1	290° F (145° C)	250° F (120° C)	cool oven
2	310° F (155° C)	275° F (135° C)	very slow oven
3	335° F (170° C)	300° F (150° C)	slow oven
4	355° F (180° C)	325° F (165° C)	very moderate oven
5	380° F (195° C)	350° F (175° C)	very moderate oven
6	400° F (205° C)	375° F (190° C)	moderate oven
7	425° F (220° C)	400° F (205° C)	moderately hot oven
8	445° F (230° C)	425° F (220° C)	hot oven
		450° F (235° C)	hot oven
9	470° F (245° C)	475° F (245° C)	very hot oven
		500° F (260° C)	very hot oven

Table of standard measures and equivalents.

American		British
appr. 7 oz (200 grams) one cup (level) sugar, granulated		8 oz = 230 grammes
appr. 5½ oz (155 grams) one cup sugar, brown, demerara		7 oz = 200 grammes
appr. 6 oz (170 grams) one cup butter or margarine		8 oz = 230 grammes
appr. 4 oz (110 grams) one cup all purpose flour (sifted)		5 oz = 140 grammes
appr. 4 oz (110 grams) one cup selfrising (selfraising) flour		5 oz = 140 grammes
appr. 7 oz (200 grams) one cup rice		10 oz = 280 grammes
appr. 5 oz (140 grams) one cup raisins (seedless)		6 oz = 165 grammes

Why all this "metric equivalent" business?
As I am sure, you will be using this book when "cooking the Dutch way" you may want to convert your recipes out of your own Dutch cookery book.
And ... as Great Britain will convert to the metric system in due time, it will be useful too.

Comparison of American and British weights and measures.
(All dry measurements are level.)
With metric equivalents given.

$cm^3 = css =$ cubic centimetres $dm^3 = 10$ decilitres $=$ litre

American
(standard cup)   metric equivalent (approximately)
1 cup = ½ pint = 8 fluid oz   = 0.237 litres
1 pint = 16 fluid oz   = 0.480 litres
¼ pint = 4 fluid oz   = 0.120 litres
1 quart = 2 pints   = 0.946 litres
1 fluid ounce   = 29,5 ccs (30 ccs)
1 (dry) ounce   = 28.35 grammes
1 pound = 16 oz   = 453 grammes
1 tablespoon = 0.50 fluid oz   = 150 ccs
1 teaspoon = 0.16 fluid oz   = 5.0 ccs

British

Soups/Soepen.

Cream soup.
Cream of tomato soup with fried
breadcubes or croutons.
Curry soup made of lima beans.
Vermicelli soup with ground
meat balls.
Dutch pea soup. Vegetable soup.

Cream soup. (Witte ragoutsoep).

2½ tbsp. butter or margarine — 6 tbsp. flour — 4 cups brown stock — 1 egg yolk — 1 tbsp. light cream — some lemon juice.
Add as accompaniment ground meat balls (see recipe of vermicelli soup).

Melt butter, add flour and stir to a smooth paste. Add stock gradually, stirring well. Bring to the boil and simmer for 5 minutes. Then remove from fire. Add some soup to egg yolk diluted with cream. Put mixture back into the soup. Stir well. Add some lemon juice to taste. Add ground meat balls if desired. They must have been cooked separately in a little water in a separate pan. The strained stock can be added to the soup if the soup is thick enough. Otherwise bind the soup with a little cornflour added to the egg yolk mixture.

Cream of tomato soup with fried bread cubes or croutons.

(Tomatensoep met gebakken broodjes).

4 cups water — 4 large tomatoes — one onion — 2 bay leaves — salt — 2 tbsp. butter or margarine — ⅓ cup flour — parsley — pepper — cream or milk.

Cut the tomatoes in four, put them into the boiling water with the sliced onion, bay leaves and salt. Simmer for 20 minutes and sieve. Melt the butter, add the flour and a little of the soup. When creamy add some more and go on till you have a creamy smooth soup. Add some finely chopped parsley, pepper and the cream or milk. Serve with fried bread cubes.

Fried bread cubes. 2 slices white bread cut in cubes, crust removed. Butter to fry them into a golden brown. Hand them round separately.

Curry soup made of lima beans.

(Kerriesoep van witte bonen).

4 cups of left-over cooking liquid and some cooked limabeans — 2 tbsp. butter or margarine — 3 cloves — 2 bay leaves — a small chili — 3 tbsp. flour — 1 tbsp. curry powder — 1 onion.

Heat the liquid and the beans. Rub through a coarse sieve. Fry the butter golden brown. Add spices except curry, then the flour and add liquid gradually. Add the curry. Serve with fried bread cubes if wanted. (see recipe cream of tomato soup page 21).

Dutch pea soup. (Erwtensoep).

2 cups split green peas — 3 qt cold water — 1 pig's trotter — 1 pig's ear — 1 cup bacon squares — 4 Frankfurters — 1 lb. potatoes — 4 tbsp. salt — 1 celeriac — 1 bunch celery-green — 2 leeks — 2 onions — salt.

Wash the peas, soak for 12 hours (unless you use quick cooking peas) and boil gently in the water they were soaked in for at least two hours. Cook in this liquid the trotter and the ear and the bacon for one hour. Add the sliced potatoes, salt diced celeriac, cut up leeks and celery leaves and cook until everything is done and the soup is smooth and thick. Add the Frankfurters for the last 10 minutes. The longer the soup simmers the better the taste. Three hours is the usual time in Holland. The soup gets so thick when it cools that it can be cut next day. The next day the soup tasts even better. That is why it is made in such big quantities.

Vegetable soup. (Groentesoep).

4 cups water — 3 bouillon cubes of 4 cups white stock (meat or bones) — 2 tbsp. quick

*boiling rice — parsley — ½ lb. carrots —
¼ cauliflower — a few Brussels sprouts —
1 stalk of celery — 1 leek — 2 tbsp. butter
or margarine — 2 bay leaves — salt.*

Dissolve the cubes into the water. Wash
the rice and add it to the water or stock.
Cook until tender. Clean and wash all
the vegetables. Cut the carrots in rounds,
the Brussels sprouts in quarters, the celery
in bits, the leek in rounds and the cauliflower in small bits. Sauté the vegetables
and the bay leaves for 15 minutes in the
butter and add the soup. Simmer for 15
minutes. Before serving, add the very

finely chopped parsley. Add salt to taste.
Instead of rice you can also take vermicelli. Break it before adding to the stock.

Vermicelli soup with ground meat balls.
(Vermicellisoep met balletjes).

*4 cups of white stock (meat or bones) — 2
blades of mace or some marjoram — ⅔ cup
of vermicelli — ½ cup ground meat (half
veal, half pork) — salt, pepper, grated
nutmeg — 1 egg.*

Make a fairly concentrated beef stock
and simmer in it the blades of mace or

marjoram. Strain and add the broken vermicelli. Prepare some small (the size of a marble) **ground meat balls** by mixing the ground meat with the salt, pepper, a little grated nutmeg and some egg. Roll them in the flour and boil in the soup for the last 15 minutes. The rest of the egg can be added to the soup just before serving, but is not essential. Add salt to taste.

Entrée dishes or lunch dishes.

Dutch Herring

Mixed herring salad

Shrimp croquettes

Meat croquettes

Meat-filled pancake

Ham and cheese savory

Kidney savories

"Chucker out"

Dutch Herring [1]).   (Hollandse haring).

The Dutch herring available in your country is more salty than it is in Holland. This is due to the fact that the preserving salt has gone through a longer permeation process. In Holland the fish is eaten almost as soon as it is brought ashore. In your country it is advisable to soak the herring in milk or water **24** hours before serving, renewing the liquid at intervals and to do this after the fish has been cleaned and skinned.

Serve Dutch herring on small toasted canapés as an appetizer, or on ice cubes, with boiled new potatoes and a green salad.

Mixed herring-salad.   (Haringsla).

1 small cooked beetroot — 2 cooking apples — some (pickled) onions and gherkins — 8 cold cooked potatoes — 2 hard boiled eggs — some lettuce or curly endives — 2 tbsp. salad oil — 2 tbsp. vinegar — salt — mayonnaise — 3 fresh salted herrings.

Soak the herrings as indicated in the

-----
[1]) Note that the herring is eaten raw and not cooked.

previous recipe. Bone the herrings and cut them up in small pieces. Keep a few pieces for decorating. Cut the peeled beetroot and apples in pieces. Chop the onions, gherkins and potatoes and one egg. Wash the lettuce or endives and shred it very finely. Put all these ingredients in a big bowl. Mix it well with salad oil, vinegar and salt. Put the salad on a flat dish and smooth the top with a

wet spoon. Coat the salad with mayonnaise and decorate with quarters of egg, pieces of herring and surround it with very small bits of "yellow" lettuce (the inside leaves). Serve it with toast and butter or, if dished up at lunchtime, with bread and butter.

Shrimp croquettes.

(Garnalen croquetjes).

1 cup cooked shrimps (prawns) — ½ envelope gelatin — 2 tbsp. flour — 2 tbsp. butter or margarine — ½ cup milk — 1 egg yolk — light cream — juice of ½ lemon — salt, pepper, chopped parsley — 2 egg whites — 1 tbsp. salad oil — dry bread crumbs — fat or oil for deep frying.

Wash and drain the shrimps. Soak gelatin in some of the cold milk. Make a thick sauce of flour, butter, milk and stock and add shrimps and gelatin. Beat the egg yolk with the cream, add the sauce and return to saucepan for thickening, taking care that it does not boil. Add lemon juice, parsley, salt and pepper. Spread this mixture onto a shallow dish to cool and set.

When set, cut in eight equal parts and

form a firm cylinder of each. Roll each in bread crumbs, then in a mixture of beaten egg whites and salad oil, then again in bread crumbs, again in egg white and bread crumbs. Fry in hot deep fat (400°) until golden brown and serve hot, garnished with some sprigs of parsley that have been fried crisp (but not brown) in the same deep fat. Serve on a platter on a doyley.

Meat croquettes. (Vleescroquetjes).

½ lb. lean veal — 1½ cups water — seasoning: a small onion, parsley, bay leaf — dry bread crumbs, egg white and fat for frying — ½ envelope gelatin — 2 tbsp. butter or margarine — 3 tbsp. flour — 1 cup veal stock — salt, pepper — lemon juice — 1 egg yolk.

Boil meat in water with seasoning until well done. Cut in very small pieces. Soak gelatin in some of the cold milk. Make a sauce of butter, flour and stock, add the gelatin, pepper and salt, lemon juice to taste and egg yolk. Add the meat. Taste. Spread this mixture onto a shallow dish. Let cool and set.
Proceed as given in the previous recipe.

Ham and cheese savories.

(Warme ham- en kaassandwiches).

8 thin slices of stale bread — 4 slices (¼ oz each) Gouda or Edam cheese — 4 slices ham (½ oz each) — butter or margarine, or dripping for frying.

Remove the crust from the bread and cut it in identical slices. Cut the cheese and the ham to the same size. Put 1 slice of ham and 1 slice of cheese between two slices of bread.

Spread the sandwiches on the outside with butter or margarine. Fry them golden brown and crisp and serve this savory either for lunch, or as an entrée, after the soup with a main meal.

Meat-filled pancake.

(Gevulde pannekoek).

For the pancakes: 1 cup flour — 1½ cups milk — 2 eggs — salt — butter or margarine for baking.
For the filling: 4 tbsp. butter or margarine —

⅓ cup flour — 2 cups stock or bouillon — salt, pepper, nutmeg, lemon juice to taste — 2 cups cooked meat, ground or minced — ½ cup canned mushrooms.

Make a thick brown sauce of butter, flour and stock: add seasoning, keep stirring and mix with meat and mushrooms. Keep hot but take care that it does not boil, or meat will get tough. Filling can be made in advance. Make smooth batter of the pancake ingredients. Heat butter in a 10-inch skillet. Use half of the batter; brown pancake slowly on one side until done. Slide onto platter and keep hot. Make second pancake in same way. Spread meat mixture on light side of first pancake and turn second pancake, brown side up, on top of first. Cut into wedges and serve at once with a green salad. Serve as a dinner entrée or for lunch.

Kidney savories. (Nierbroodjes).

1 large calf's kidney — 2 tbsp. chopped onions — 1 tbsp. butter or margarine — salt — 2 tbsp. flour — ⅔ cup stock — Worcestershire sauce — pepper — 4 slices stale white bread — 1 egg, beaten — 1 tbsp. milk — ¼ cup dry bread crumbs — fat for frying — parsley.

Wash and clean kidney. Parboil in water for one minute. Discard the water. Chop kidney very finely. Sauté onions in the butter, add kidney before onions brown. Add salt and continue frying until light brown. Sprinkle flour over the mixture and gradually add the stock. Cover and allow to simmer very slowly for 15 minutes. Add Worcestershire sauce and pepper. Taste and set aside to cool. Cut slices in half. Heap kidney mixture on bread. Put the egg in a deep plate. Stand the pieces of bread in the plate. Baste thoroughly. Coat with bread crumbs. Have deep fat ready 360°—370° F. (180° C.) and fry the savories until golden brown. Serve on a doyley on a platter. Garnish with fresh parsley sprigs.

Chucker out. (Uitsmijter).

A "uitsmijter" is a dish, ordered mostly in a small restaurant, when one is in a hurry but wants to eat something substantial.

It consists of 1 or 2 slices of white bread, buttered, topped with a liberal portion of cold, cooked thinly sliced roastbeaf or ham or veal. And on top of this two fried eggs (with one egg it is called a "halve" (half) uitsmijter).

I can recommend you this when you ransack the refrigerator and find eggs and meat. You will certainly find some bread in the bread-bin.

Poultry and game.

Stewed rabbit

Curried chicken-fricassee

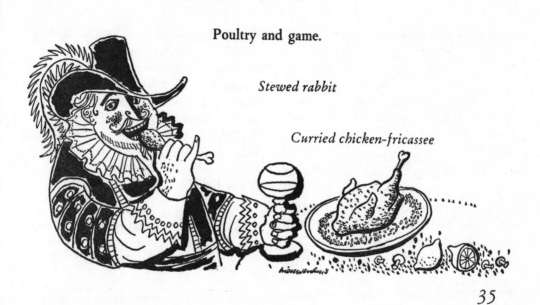

Curried chicken-fricassee.

(Kip met kerriesaus).

One cut-up chicken — salt — ⅓ cup butter or margarine — 1 teaspoon curry or more to taste — 1 medium chopped onion — 2 cups chicken broth — 1 cup fresh mushrooms — 3 tbsp. flour — milk.

Salt the chicken parts and fry in butter on all sides in a large skillet or Dutch oven. Add curry and onion 5 minutes before the frying is done and fry to a golden brown. Add the broth, cover and leave to simmer until chicken is cooked.

Cook mushrooms no longer than ten minutes in this mixture.
Remove the chicken and the mushrooms. Strain the liquid and thicken it with the flour which has been mixed with some milk beforehand. Replace the chicken and the mushrooms in this sauce and heat. Serve in a rice ring (rijstrand).

Stewed rabbit. (Gestoofd konijn).

One cut-up rabbit — ⅓ cup butter or margarine — 1 large onion, chopped — pepper, salt, bay leaves, thyme, small hot chili, parsley, celery, carrot, all chopped — 1 lemon.

*For the sauce: 2 cups stock or bouillon —
¼ cup butter or margarine — 3 tbsp. flour
— 1 tbsp. tomato paste — 1 large chopped
onion — seasoning and chopped vegetables as
for rabbit above.*

Rub rabbit pieces with pepper and salt
and brown in butter on all sides. Add
onion, seasoning, chopped vegetables and
some water. Cover and simmer one hour
or until half done.

Meanwhile make the sauce. Fry onion,
bay leaf, thyme and chili in butter.
Remove from skillet with skimmer,
leaving the butter. Add flour and brown
slightly, stirring constantly. Then add
stock, tomato paste, pepper and salt and
cook for 10 minutes. Pour sauce over
rabbit and cook one more hour or until
meat falls from bone. Add lemon juice.
Serve with rice or mashed potatoes and
with a side dish of either tomato salad,
cabbage or Brussels sprouts.

Potatoes.

Boiled potatoes
Dutch mashed potatoes
Home-fried potatoes
Potato salad

38

Boiled potatoes.

(Gekookte aardappelen).

The Dutch are very particular about the texture of their boiled potatoes. They eat quite a lot of them with their evening meal. Potatoes must be flaky when dished up.

2 lb. potatoes — 1 cup of water — salt.

Peel the potatoes, remove the eyes and put the potatoes at once into cold water. Put ½ inch of water in a saucepan with a tightly fitting lid. Add the potatoes and the salt. Bring quickly to the boil and then turn gas or electric hotplate down, as low as possible just keeping the steam *under* the lid of the pan. Cook for 20 minutes, drain and shake well until dry and flaky.

Dutch mashed potatoes.

(Aardappelpuree).

Always make nice and white mashed potatoes from freshly boiled potatoes. If

39

made from cold boiled potatoes the colour of the mashed potatoes is not white.

2 lb. potatoes — 1½ cup milk — grated nutmeg — ¼ cup butter or margarine — salt.

Boil the peeled potatoes. Mash them when still warm with a fork or put them through a mincer or through a sieve. There must not be any lumps in them. Bring the milk, nutmeg, butter or margarine and salt to the boil. Add the mashed potatoes at once and stir well. Then, with a wooden spoon, whip the mixture well until it is white and creamy, and serve, or put it into a casserole, dot with some butter and brown under the grill or in the oven.

Home-fried potatoes.
(Gebakken aardappelen).

2 lb. boiled potatoes — ¼ cup butter, margarine or cooking fat.

Cut the potatoes in slices and fry in the butter until they are golden brown. Turn them frequently with a spatula.

Potato Salad. (Aardappelsla).

1 tbsp. mustard powder — ½ onion — 2 tbsp. vinegar — mayonnaise — 3 tbsp. chopped parsley — 1 cup french dressing — 3 cups cold boiled potatoes — salt — pepper.

Mix the mustard with the chopped onion, vinegar, mayonnaise and parsley and dressing in a bowl. Slice the potatoes and stir carefully through the sauce, adding salt and pepper to taste.

Meat.

Real Dutch steak

Large meat balls

Stuffed veal- or beeffrissoles

Veal slices

Pork slices

Pickled beef

Casserole dishes.

Hunter's dish
Meat and potato casserole
Curried-rice and meat casserole
Savory beef and onion stew

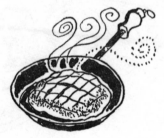

Real Dutch steak. (Hollandse biefstuk).

for 4 people: one piece of 1 lb very tender lean steak (fillet steak or tenderloin) or 4 pieces of 4 oz each — salt — pepper — milk — butter (no margarine).

Scrape (do not wash) the meat. Rub it with salt and pepper. Melt butter in skillet. Add meat when the "skum" of melting butter disappears and the butter is very hot. Put the meat into the butter, do not use a fork but two spoons (the juice must be sealed into the meat and the prongs of a fork may make holes in the meat out of which the juice will "ooze") and sear the meat on one side, then on the other side. Brown on both sides. Keep moving. The Dutch eat their "biefstuk" very rare, but if you do not like underdone meat, fry it a little longer. Then take the meat out of the pan. Keep it hot. Pour one tbsp. milk in the pan, reheat and let the gravy thicken a little. Pour over meat.

Serve with home-fried potatoes (see recipe page 40) and a salad (lettuce).

Large meat balls. (Gehakt).

½ lb. ground beef — ½ lb. ground pork —
4 slices stale bread — ½ cup milk — 1 tbps.
salt — bread crumbs — ½ tsp. nutmeg —
pinch of pepper — ½ onion — ¼ cup margarine or fat — 1 tsp. tomato-paste or 1 tbsp.
tomato juice.

Mix the meat in a large basin. Remove
the crusts from the bread and soak in
the milk. Fry the chopped onion in some
fat. Mix this all together with salt, pepper
and nutmeg. Shape into 4 or 8 balls. Roll
through flour and fry them until brown
in the fat. Add some water and simmer
for 15 minutes. Add tomato paste to
gravy. Serve with boiled potatoes and
boiled vegetables.

Stuffed veal- or beefrissoles.
(Blinde vinken).

4 thin slices veal or beef, 2 oz each — 2 large
slices of bread — some milk — salt — pinch
of nutmeg — 2 oz ground veal or beef or
sausage meat — 1 egg — 4 thin slices lean
bacon — cotton thread or cocktailsticks —
1 tsp. cooking oil — bread crumbs or Dutch
rusks — butter or margarine.

Crumble the bread and soak it in milk until soft. Make it into a smooth paste with a fork. Add salt, grated nutmeg and ground meat. Work it into a firm mixture in which no lumps of bread may be noticeable. Separate the egg. Brush every slice of meat with a little unbeaten white of egg and coat this side with a slice of bacon and some ground meat-paste. Roll up and secure the meat with some cotton or stick two cocktailsticks in the part where the meat joins. Put rest of white of egg, the yolk and the cooking oil in a deep plate. Mix it with a fork. Put some bread crumbs or finely ground rusks on a piece of greaseproof paper. Put the "rissoles" through egg, roll them in bread crumbs or rusks crumbs and melt some butter or margarine in a shallow pan or Dutch oven until golden brown. Put the meat into the fat, fry to a golden brown, then add very little water. Cover the pan and simmer for 20 minutes, (beefrissoles for 1 hour). Carefully remove the threads or the cocktailsticks, use the sauce as a gravy over e.g. mashed potatoes (see recipe page 39).

Veal slices. (Kalfslapjes).

4 thin slices of lean veal — salt — bread-crumbs or Dutch rusks — ½ cup butter or margarine — 1 lemon.

Wash the meat and season it with salt. Coat it in bread crumbs or finely ground rusks. Melt the butter or margarine in a frying pan until brown and fry the veal slices in the butter, browning them on both sides. Cook slowly, without a lid on the pan for 20 minutes. Turn the slices occasionally. Then take them out of the frying pan. Keep them hot.

Make the **Dutch gravy** (jus) by adding 3 tbsp. water. Good gravy should be ⅓ fat and ⅔ brown stock.
Serve the veal slices with a slice of lemon on top and serve the gravy with boiled potatoes.

Pork chops. (Varkenscarbonades).

4 pork chops — pepper — salt — butter or margarine.

Fry the chops. Cook over low heat 35—40 minutes until tender.
Serve with potatoes and Brussels sprouts.

Pickled beef. (Runderlappen).

1½ lb. lean stewing beef (cut in four steaks) — pepper — salt — 6 tbsp. butter or bacon drippings — 1 large onion — 1½ tbsp. vinegar — 1 tsp. mustard — 1 bay leaf — some cloves and peppercorns.

Scrape the meat and rub with pepper and salt. Heat butter or fat in a skillet or Dutch oven until it is real hot and thoroughly brown the meat on both sides. Add the sliced onion at the last moment, fry them very lightly without getting brown. Dissolve the remainder in the pan with some water and pour it over the meat. Add vinegar, mustard and the herbs; cover and allow to simmer very gently for about two to three hours, or until very soft, while turning every half hour.

Serve the meat with mashed potatoes (see recipe page 39). Strain the sauce if desired and pour over the meat. Red cabbage is a favorite vegetable with this dish, or spinach, or chicory.

Hunter's dish. (Jachtschotel).

As much cold meat as available — ½ lb.

47

cooking apples — 3 medium onions, peeled and sliced very thin — 3 tbsp. butter or margarine — 12 big boiled potatoes — pepper — salt — 1 cup stock or bouillon made from meat cubes.

Slice the meat, peel the apples, slice them. Fry them with the onions until golden brown.

Arrange alternate layers of sliced potatoes, meat, onions and apples in a casserole. Season with pepper and salt. Take care that the last layer will be of potatoes, but do not put it on top yet. Pour the stock over the contents of the dish.

Finish off with potatoes. Dot with butter. Put in the oven until thoroughly hot and brown on top.

Serve with spiced red cabbage or with stewed sliced (cooked) beetroots (see page 58) or thick applesauce.

Meat and potato casserole.

(Lit. Philosopher's dish). (Filosoof).

½ lb. cold meat — 1 lb. boiled potatoes — 2 tbsp. butter or margarine — 1 cup gravy and water or stock — 1 small onion — pepper — salt — nutmeg — bread crumbs — butter.

Mince the meat, mash the potatoes, fry the chopped onion in the butter. Mix all these ingredients together and add the gravy or stock until it is as thick as mashed potatoes. Sprinkle in some pepper, salt and nutmeg. Put in a casserole, cover with bread crumbs, and some knobs of butter. Heat and brown in the oven or under the grill.

Curried rice and meat casserole.

(Kerrieschoteltje).

2 big minced onions — ½ tbsp. currypowder — 1 cup or more minced leftover pork meat — 1 cup uncooked quick boiling or 3 cups cooked rice — salt — 2 cups meat stock.

Melt the butter in a skillet, add the onions and curry. Fry to a golden brown. Add meat, rice (always cooked), salt and stock. Heat thoroughly. Serve with a green salad.

Savory beef and onion stew.
(Hachée).

2 large thinly sliced onions — ¼ cup flour — ¼ cup butter or margarine — 2 cups stock or stock of meatcubes — 3 bay leaves — 5 cloves — 1 tbsp. vinegar — ½ lb. sliced cold or leftover meat, preferably beef — 2 tbsp. cornflour — pepper — Worcestershire sauce.

Brown the onions and the flour in the butter in a saucepan. Add stock gradually, stirring all the time. Add bay leaves and cloves and simmer for five minutes with the lid on the pan. Add the vinegar and the diced meat, simmer for another hour. Mix the cornflour with a little water, add this to the stew to thicken the sauce. Simmer for 5 minutes, stirring continuously. Make it to taste with a little pepper and Worcestershire sauce.

Serve with mashed or boiled potatoes and red cabbage (see recipe page 39 and page 58) with this dish.

Fish.

Fried fish

Stewed eel

Flounder or sole with shrimps

Cod-fish and rice dish

Casserole dishes.

Dutch fish casserole

Fish casserole with mustard sauce

Fried fish. (Gebakken vis).

Fish for frying may be: any fillet — whiting — haddock and the like — cooking oil.

Fry the cleaned and seasoned fish in a skillet with cooking oil ⅛ inch deep. Either dip in flour or in milk. Sprinkle with lemon when cooked. Serve with home-fried potatoes (see recipe page 40) and a green salad. Haddock may be served with stewed beetroots.

Stewed Eel. (Gestoofde paling).

1½ lb. eel — ¼ cup butter or margarine — salt — water — lemon — bread crumbs.

Cut the skinned eel in slices, clean and wash them, salt the slices and put them in a casserole dish. Add a little water, lemon juice and butter. Sprinkle bread crumbs over the fish, bake in a hot oven, with the lid on, for 15 or 20 minutes. Lower temperature, remove lid and cook for a further 10 minutes. Serve with boiled potatoes and a green salad.

Flounder or sole with shrimps.
(Tongfilet met garnalen).

*1 lb. fillets of flounder or sole — salt — 3
tbsp. butter or margarine — 2 tbsp. flour —
1½ cup fish-stock — juice of one lemon or
equal quantity of white wine — 1 egg yolk —
¼ cup of cream or milk — ¼ cup washed
shrimps — parsley — lemon wedges.*

Tie each fillet in a knot. Boil the fish in
about two cups of salted water or
"court bouillon" (fish-stock to which
some white wine is added), until just
done but still whole. Make a thick sauce
of butter, flour and stock — add lemon
juice or wine and then carefully the egg
yolk and the cream or milk. Heat the
fish and the shrimps in this sauce and
sprinkle with parsley.
Decorate with parsley sprigs and lemon
wedges.

Cod-fish and rice dish.
(Stokvisschotel).

*2 lb. soaked dried codfish, shredded — 1 or
1½ tbsp. salt — 1½ lb. potatoes — 3 cups of
uncooked (quick-boiling) rice — ½ lb. chopped*

onions — ½ cup butter or margarine — 2½ tbsp. flour — mustard.

Tie up dried fish in rolls and cook in salted water to cover. Simmer gently to prevent it getting hard. Cooking time 1—1½ hours. Turn out on serving dish. Peel potatoes and boil in little salted water (30 minutes). Turn out on dish. Boil rice, dry and turn out. Fry onions in some fat until light brown. Prepare mustard sauce from 1½ cup broth (fish stock), the butter or margarine, the flour, salt and a spoonful of mustard.

Serve separately with the other dishes. Eat out of a soup plate. Mix everything in the plate and eat with a dessert or soup spoon. Serve with melted butter.

Dutch fish casserole. (Panvis).

The same ingredients as above. Same preparations but place mixture of all the ingredients in a casserole. If too dry add some water the fish has been boiled in. Sprinkle with bread crumbs, dot with butter. Place in oven to heat and brown. Serve with a salad.

Fish casserole with mustard sauce.

(Visschotel met mosterdsaus)

*For the casserole: 2 large sliced onions —
2 tbsp. butter or margarine — 1 lb. boiled
or leftover fish (whiting, cod, plaice or frozen
fish) — lemon juice — leftover Dutch mashed
potatoes (see recipe page 39).*

*For the mustard sauce: 1½ cup of fish stock
(if leftover, otherwise take 1½ cup of water
and 1 meatcube) — a scant ½ cup flour —
2 tbsp. butter or margarine — mustard. (In
Holland we use made-up mustard.)*

Bring the fish stock or water to the boil. Mix the flour with a little water to a smooth paste and pour into the sauce liquid, stir until it thickens. Add the butter or margarine and the mustard. Fry the onions to a golden brown. Put the bits of fish on the bottom of a casserole. Sprinkle some lemon juice on them. Alternate with mashed potatoes, onions, fish and mustard sauce, until all the ingredients are used up and finish with a layer of mashed potatoes. Put the dish in the oven to heat and brown on top.

Casserole dishes.

Chicory dishes
Cabbage and meat balls casserole
Brown beans and bacon
Hotchpotch
Curly kale and sausages

Vegetables.

Stewed beetroot
Spiced red cabbage
Spinach with hard boiled eggs

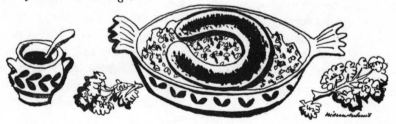

Stewed beetroot. (Gestoofde bieten).

1½ lb. cooked beetroot — 1 small onion — salt — 1 tsp. sugar — 3 cloves — dash of vinegar — knob of butter or margarine — 2 tsp. cornflour.

Peel (slip off skins) the beetroots and slice them. Put them in a saucepan with a little water, chopped onion, salt, sugar, cloves, vinegar and butter or margarine. Simmer them for ten minutes (keep the lid on the pan). Bind the liquid at the last moment with a little cornflour, made into a paste of pouring consistency with some cold water.

Spiced red cabbage. (Rode kool).

One small red cabbage — ¼ cup of butter or margarine — 3 cloves — 2 cooking apples — 1 tbsp. sugar — some vinegar, if liked — salt.

Remove the outer leaves of the cabbage. Cut the cabbage in halves. Remove the core. Wash and shred cabbage very thinly. Put a little butter or margarine in a saucepan and 1 cup of water. Add the red cabbage, the cloves, the peeled, cored and sliced apples and simmer the vegetables with a tight fitting lid on the pan for ¾ hour. Then add the rest of the butter or margarine, the sugar, some vinegar and simmer for another 5 minutes.

Spinach and hard-boiled eggs.

(Spinazie met harde eieren).

4 lb. spinach — salt — 2 tbsp. flour — 2 tbsp. butter or margarine — 8 fingers of bread — 2 eggs — butter to fry bread in.

Pick and wash spinach, add salt and cook without water. Toss spinach after it has boiled a few minutes. Cook for 5 to 10 minutes. Drain, cut or chop up spinach, stir in flour and add butter. Boil up to thicken. Fry fingers of bread in butter and hard-boil the eggs. Decorate spinach with fried bread (standing upright) and eggs cut in eight.

Chicory or endives with cheese sauce.

(Brussels lof met kaassaus).

2 lb. of chicory — salt.
For the cheese sauce: 3 tbsp. butter or margarine — a scant ½ cup flour — 1½ cup half

milk, half water or some stock made from 2 meatcubes — ½ cup grated Gouda cheese — Worcestershire sauce — salt — pepper.

Cut a very thin piece from the bottom of the chicory. Then insert a pointed vegetable knife and remove the core, which is rather bitter. Wash the vegetable and boil it for 20 minutes in salted water, or until tender. Then drain it well, put it in a casserole and cover the chicory with a cheese sauce made as follows:
melt the butter or margarine, add the flour and blend into a smooth paste. Then add the milk, water and meatcube-stock stirring well. Boil for 5 minutes and add the grated cheese off the fire. Make it to taste with a little Worcestershire sauce and some salt and pepper. Cover the vegetable with it and put in the oven to color to a golden brown. **(Brussels lof met ham.)**
A variation is: boil the chicory heads. Drain and wrap each head in a slice of ham. Put in a casserole. Cover with thick cheese sauce and put into the oven to brown.
And a second one: Cook them, drain

well. Hard-boil one egg a head. Peel. Cut into halves (lengthwise). Melt some butter. Serve chicory on a hot plate. Decorate with eggs and hand round the butter and some grated nutmeg separately. **(Brussels lof met eieren.)**

Cabbage and meat balls casserole.
(Koolschotel met gehakt).

1 head of cabbage — 1 lb. ground beef or pork, prepared for meat loaf according to preference — mashed potatoes. (See recipe page 39).

Clean and shred the cabbage and boil until almost done ($\frac{3}{4}$ hour). Drain well. Meanwhile roll meat loaf ingredients into balls, brown them in butter in open skillet. Add a little water and simmer until done. Prepare the mashed potatoes. Place half of the cabbage in a casserole, top with the meat balls and cover with the remainder of the cabbage. Pour some of the gravy over the dish. Cover with the mashed potatoes. Dot with butter and brown in hot oven.

Brown beans (kidney beans) and bacon.
(Bruine bonen met spek).

1 cup brown beans — bacon — salt — onions.

Wash beans in ample water, soak overnight and boil in soaking water. Add salt when beans are nearly done. Cooking time ¾—1 hour. Clean bacon, cut into strips or squares and fry slowly until brown. Clean onions, cut in pieces, fry in bacon dripping. Use dripping as a sauce. Serve with boiled potatoes (see recipe page 39) and thick apple sauce (appelmoes).

Hotchpotch. (Hutspot met klapstuk).

1 lb. lean boneless chuck (thin flank) — salt — ⅔ lb. onions — 4 lb. potatoes — 2 lb. carrots — milk — 4 tbsp. fat, butter or margarine — pepper.

Wash meat, boil in 2 cups water and salt for about two hours. Scrub and mince carrots. Peel, wash and slice onions and add them to the meat together with peeled and cut potatoes and carrots. Boil until done (about 30 minutes). Remove meat from pan. Mash all the vegetables and add fat, butter or margarine and pepper. If too thick add some milk (but a spoon must stand up in it). Serve with the sliced meat. This dish is eaten as a main meal dish, either with some soup to start, and followed up with fruit, as the dish is very nourishing. This amount serves 4 people in Holland (they have big appetites).

Curly kale and sausages.
(Stamppot van boerenkool met worst).

2 or 3 lb. curly kale — 3 lb. potatoes — milk — salt — about 1 lb. smoked sausage or Frankfurters — 4 tbsp. fat, butter or margarine — pepper.

Strip, wash and cut up the kale very finely. Boil kale in little boiling water with salt, about 40 minutes. Add peeled and cut potatoes and sausage and enough water to prevent burning (cooking time 30 minutes). Remove sausage from pan, mash remainder and stir in boiled milk until smooth. Taste, add some pepper if desired.

"Stamppot" means that the vegetables and potatoes are mixed to a smooth consistency. It is a typical winterdish at home and the Dutch have a saying: never eat curly kale before the frost has got at it.

Hot puddings.

Holland drop-scones

Cinnamon turn-overs

Real Holland pancakes

Ordinary pancakes

Apple pancakes

Bacon pancakes
Dutch doughnuts
Snowballs

Steamed puddings.

Steamed sultana pudding,

with molasses or sauce

(golden syrup)

John in the sack

65

Holland Drop-scones. (Drie in de pan).

Drie in de pan means: Three-in-the (frying) pan. The Dutch make them mostly of a yeast dough a little thinner than for Dutch doughnuts. But they can also be made of self-rising flour:

2 cups self-rising flour — salt — 1 egg — 1½ cup lukewarm milk — 1 cup mixed currants and raisins (washed) — butter, margarine or cooking oil for frying — sugar.

Put the flour and the salt into a bowl, make a well in the centre. Put in the egg and 1 cup milk. Mix to a smooth batter. Add rest of milk and fruit. Then melt butter or oil in heavy skillet. Drop three pancakes into the hot fat and fry them on both sides to a golden brown. Turn them when puffed and full of bubbles (as you do griddle cakes or scones). Serve hot with sugar.

Cinnamon turn-overs. (Wentelteefjes).

8 slices stale bread — 1 tsp. ground cinnamon — sugar — 1 egg — 1½ cup milk — pinch of salt — butter or margarine to fry.

Take the crusts off the bread. Stir cinnamon and sugar together. Add the beaten egg and milk, also the salt. Soak the slices in this mixture. Fry them slowly in butter on both sides and sprinkle with sugar before serving.

Real Holland Pancakes.

(Eierpannekoeken)

These pancakes are as big as a dinner plate and formerly even bigger (12″ in diameter!). Nowadays you may find such big pancakes on the menu of a restaurant, but at home we make them the dinner plate size. They are either eaten as a savory (with smoked sausage or bacon) or as a sweet (plain with molasses or golden syrup or with apples). Pancakes are best when made with yeast and they should be served piping hot. Use two skillets when available. Keep the pancakes hot on steam, or covered in the oven. Cold pancakes are awful! The following recipe is a luxury one, for special occasions, as many eggs are used in preparing (in stead of yeast).

For one large pancake: 1 cup flour — salt — 2 large eggs or 3 medium (½ cup beaten) — 1 cup milk — at least ¼ cup butter or margarine.

Put the flour and the salt in a bowl, make a well in the middle and add the beaten eggs. Mix to a smooth batter. Add the rest of the milk. Melt half the butter in a heavy skillet. Pour the batter into it. Turn these pancakes frequently, each time adding some butter. They should then become golden brown and crisp at the sides.

Ordinary pancakes.   (makes 4 big ones).

Gewone pannekoeken.

(Voldoende voor 4 grote koeken).

4 cups flour or 4 cups Aunt Jemima pancake mix — salt — 1 cake yeast (⅗ oz) — 4 cups lukewarm milk — butter or margarine.

Put the flour and the salt in a bowl. Make a well in the centre. Add the diluted (with a little milk) yeast. Add 2 cups milk and mix to a smooth batter. Add the rest of the milk. Leave to rise for ¾ hour. Heat enough butter in a heavy skillet. Pour in part of the butter and fry the pancake on both sides. (You can toss the pancake in the air for turning, if you like. Otherwise use a spatula). Keep them hot and serve with sugar or molasses, golden syrup or treacle.

Apple pancakes. (Appelpannekoeken).

The above recipe and a small tart (cooking) apple for each pancake — brown sugar — cinnamon.

Make the batter. Core, peel and slice the apples. When baking the pancake put 3 or 4 slices on top and cook them in the batter. Serve with sugar or brown sugar and some cinnamon, if liked.

Bacon pancakes. (Spekpannekoeken).

Ordinary pancake recipe (see page 68)

(without butter or margarine) — 3 oz bacon rashers. Serve with brown sugar or molasses, treacle or golden syrup.

Make the batter. Meanwhile fry the bacon in the skillet until crisp. Divide into as many portions as pancakes required. Also pour dripping out of the pan. Use for frying next pancake.

Put the bacon on the bottom of the pan. Pour batter on top. Bake the pancakes until crisp at the sides and golden brown. Toss (turn) once or twice.

Dutch doughnuts. (makes 20)
(Oliebollen).

1 cake yeast (⅔ oz) — 1 cup milk — 2¼ cups flour — 2 tsp. salt — 1 egg — 1½ cups currants and raisins (washed) — 1 tart (cooking) apple — fat for deep frying.

First blend the yeast with a little luke-warm milk. Sift the flour and salt. Add milk, mix to a batter with yeast and egg. Add currants, raisins and peeled, minced apple. Leave batter in a warm place to rise to double its size. Heat the fat to 375° F. (190° C.). Put two metal spoons into the batter. Shape balls with the two spoons and drop them into the fat. Fry them for 8 minutes until brown. The doughnuts should be soft and should not be grease-soaked inside. If they are fried too slowly the crust becomes hard and tough and the doughnuts become greasy. Drain on absorbent paper. Serve then piled on a dish and cover thickly with sifted confectioner's sugar. Eat them hot, if possible.

"Oliebollen" are a traditional treat on New Year's Eve in Holland.

Snowballs. (makes 20).
(Sneeuwballen).

½ *cup cold water — salt — ½ cup butter or margarine — 10 tbsp. flour, sifted — 2 eggs — 2 tbsp. washed, dried currants or sultanas or raisins — cooking oil or fat for frying — sifted confectioner's sugar.*

Mix water, salt and butter and bring to the boil. Remove from heat and stir in flour. Put back on heat. Keep stirring with wooden spoon until mixture leaves the pan and forms a ball. Remove from heat. Cool and then break in the eggs one at a time, beating well until smooth. Add the currants and raisins. Heat fresh oil or fat to 360°—370° F. (180° C.) and with a metal tablespoon (which should be dipped in the hot oil first) take out a spoonful of batter and fry until golden brown on both sides. This takes about ten minutes. These will puff up and become very light. Watch the temperature of the fat. Drain on brown paper and sprinkle with confectioner's sugar.

These "Snowballs" are also a traditional New Year's Eve sweet. They can also be made without the fruit. Then they must be cut open at the side and filled with sweetened whipped cream.

Steamed sultana pudding with molasses or treacle sauce.
(Ketelkoek met stroopsaus)

For the pudding: 2½ cup self rising flour —
1 cup milk — 1 egg — salt — ½ cup each currants and raisins, washed — butter or margarine — bread crumbs or ground Dutch rusks.

For the sauce: 1 cup molasses or treacle (Brown treacle, if possible) — 3 tbsp. butter or margarine — a dash of cinnamon.

Wash the fruit. Dry it in a towel. Grease a pudding-basin or a tube centre mold. Also grease the lid. Coat both with bread crumbs or ground Dutch rusks. Beat the egg, mix in the flour, the milk, salt and fruit. Mix to a smooth batter. Pour it into the basin (which may be ¾ filled only) and close tightly. Lay waxed paper loosely over tube centre mold if used. Cook for two hours in boiling water. When cooked take it out of the basin, turn it on to a big plate and dry it a moment under the grill. Make the molasses or treacle sauce: slowly melt the molasses or treacle and the butter or margarine over a low fire, put it in a gravy boat. Serve the pudding in slices and pour the sauce over it. This pudding, when left over and cold, can be eaten for tea, with butter or margarine and sugar, or spread with butter or margarine and treacle.

John in the sack. (A Dutch steamed pudding like roly-poly). (Jan in de zak).

1 cake compressed yeast (⅔ oz) — ¼ cup lukewarm water — 3 cups sifted flour — 1 egg — salt — ¾ cup milk, scalded and cooled to lukewarm — ⅓ cup each of raisins and currants (washed) — chopped peel.

Sprinkle yeast into lukewarm water and stir until dissolved. Place flour in bowl, add egg and milk, stir with wooden spoon until flour absorbs liquid. Then add fruit and salt and mix well. Add the yeast-water mixture and blend well with wooden spoon (dough will be sticky). Place dough in bowl, cover and let rise in a warm place for 45 minutes. Meanwhile sprinkle a clean wet cloth with flour. Roll dough into an oblong and tie loosely into cloth, filling two thirds full. Firmly fasten ends, stick safety pin in the middle. Steam 2 to 3 hours. Remove from cloth and serve hot with a molasses (treacle) sauce or with melted butter and brown sugar. Do not cut with a knife, but with a piece of string. If served cold, the next day, sprinkle with sugar and spread with butter.

"John in the sack" derives its odd name from the fact that it used to be made in a clean white pillow case, instead of in a mold. (Nowadays we use a linen cloth).

Desserts (Sweets)   and   Puddings.

The Hague bluff	*Chocolate custard*
Yoghurt cream with fresh fruits	*Black and white custard*
Bread porridge	*Chipolata pudding*
Hang-up	

Dutch rusks with red currant sauce

Farina (semolina) cream with sultanas

Rice with currants

*Farina (semolina) pudding with
red currant sauce*

The Hague Bluff. (Haagse bluf).

The good citizens of the Hague are often accused by their countrymen — rightly or wrongly so — of bragging or showing off. The following recipe, "The Hague Bluff" is so named because it produces quite a fluffy dessert out of practically nothing. It is a great favourite with Dutch children.

3 tablespoons raspberry syrup — ½ cup sugar — one egg white.

Put raspberry syrup, sugar and the unbeaten white of egg in a deep bowl or in an electric-mixer. Beat by hand ten minutes or more, the idea being that the longer one beats, the more one gets. Serve with a wafer or lady finger.

In Holland it is made of red currant juice, but I believe that this is not available in the shops in England and America. That's why I chose raspberry syrup as a substitute.

Yoghurt cream with fresh fruit.

(Yoghurtvla met vruchten).

4 cups yoghurt (yoghurt in Holland is rather thin, like custard. Hence 4 cups of it.) — 1 package instant vanilla pie filling — 4 cups milk — ½ lb. fruit in season — sugar to taste.

Wash the fruit and place in a glass bowl and cover with sugar to taste. Leave sugar to permeate for a couple of hours.
Take enough pudding powder to mix with 4 cups of milk and prepare according to indication on package. Chill. Mix well with chilled yoghurt and pour over fruit just before serving. Decorate with some well chosen fruits and serve with wafers or lady fingers.
Instead of yoghurt the "Hang-up" recipe can be used. Only the "Hang-up" should be very thick and left to drip much longer (see recipe page 79).

Bread porridge. (Broodpap).

4 cups milk — 4 slices stale bread cut in dice — ½ cup of brown sugar — 2 tbsp. of ground cinnamon — 1 tbsp. butter or margarine.

Bring the milk except for a few spoonfuls to the boil. Add the bread. Boil for ten minutes. Mix the sugar with the cinnamon and stir into the milk. Add the butter at the last moment.

Hang up. (Hangop). In Britain it resembles Bonny Clabber.

This Dutch dessert is popular with the housewives, for it is the easiest thing to make.

2 quarts buttermilk (8 cups) — sugar to taste — ground cinnamon — 1 Dutch rusk per person or some crackers.

Place a clean, wet cloth in a strainer or colander. Pour the buttermilk into the cloth. Leave it there to drip for at least two hours, or until the residue in the cloth is as thick as unwhipped cream. Stir and scrape it off the cloth from time to time in order to allow the whey to drip away freely. Now scoop the stiff cream of the buttermilk off the cloth into a bowl and whip with a whisk until all lumps are removed. Add sugar to taste and chill. Serve in a soup plate with ground cinnamon and coarsely crumbled Dutch rusks, which are sprinkled on top.

This dessert is called Hang up, because in former days the buttermilk was poured into a wet linen pillow case and hung up by a string above the sink. The name has stuck and some people still make it that way.

Farina (semolina) cream with sultanas.
(Griesmeelpap met rozijnen).

4 cups milk — ⅔ cup sultanas — a pinch of salt — 3 oz. farina — 4 tbsp. sugar — ½ tbsp. butter or margarine.

Bring the milk to the boil with washed sultanas and the salt. Mix sugar and farina thoroughly and stir into the boiling milk. Boil gently 5—20 minutes (the coarser the cereal, the longer the cooking time). Add butter. Eat out of a deep plate.

Rice with currants. (Rijst met krenten).

1½ cup (quick-boiling) rice — 1½ cup currants — 4 cups water — ½ tsp. salt — lemon rind — butter or margarine — sugar.

Wash the rice and currants well and cook together in the water. Add salt and lemon rind. Serve with butter and sugar.

Dutch rusks with red currant sauce.

(Beschuit met bessensap).

6 tbsp. red currant jelly — ½ cup boiling water — 1 cup water — 4 Dutch rusks — 1 stick cinnamon — peel of 1 lemon — 2 tbsp. cornflour.

Dilute 3 tbsp. of jelly with the boiling water. Put the rusks in a shallow, oblong dish and soak them in the liquid. Bring the rest of the jelly, water, cinnamon and lemon peel to the boil in a covered saucepan and leave to simmer for a while. Mix the cornflour with a little cold water to a pouring consistency. Remove the cinnamon and the peel and thicken the red currant jelly sauce with the cornflour without boiling it. Pour the sauce over the rusks and serve either hot or cold.

Farina (semolina) pudding with red currant sauce.

(Griesmeelpudding met bessensap).

For the pudding: 4 cups milk — vanilla essence to taste — ⅔ cup farina — 2 tbsp. cornflour — ¼ cup sugar — pinch of salt — 1½ tbsp. butter — 1 egg yolk beaten and one egg white beaten stiff.

Boil the milk with vanilla. Add mixture of farina, cornflour, sugar and salt.

stirring vigorously. Turn the heat to low; add butter and then the egg yolk carefully. Then fold in the beaten egg white. Pour pudding into a mould rinsed with cold water and chill.

For the sauce: Jar of red currant jelly — juice of two lemons — ½ cup boiling water.

Place currant jelly in a saucepan. Add lemon and boiling water, bring to a boil and stir until smooth. Chill.

Turn the pudding onto a platter and surround it with part of the sauce. Serve the rest separately in a gravy-boat. The thickness of the "griesmeelpudding" can be adapted to taste by altering the amount of farina given above. In Holland it is generally preferred quite thick.

Chocolate custard. (Chocoladevla)

3 cups milk — 3 tbsp. cornflour — 1 oz or square unsweetened chocolate or 1 oz cocoa — 6 tbsp. sugar — a pinch of salt — whipped cream (sweetened).

Bring the milk except for a few spoonfuls, to the boil. Mix the cornflour, chocolate and sugar dry and smooth out the lumps. Then add the cold milk and blend smoothly. Pour into the boiling milk, add the salt and boil stirring well, for three minutes. Let cool, stir to prevent forming a skin. Pour in a shallow glass dish and top with sweetened cream.

Black and white custard. (Zwart-wit vla of crème panachée).

Vanilla flavored custard and chocolate custard of even texture. Holding one pan in your left hand and the other in your right pour both custards, evenly into a shallow glass dish. Top with cream.

Chipolata pudding. (Chipolata pudding)

½ oz or 1½ envelope gelatin — 1 oz lady fingers — 3 tbsp. Marasquino liqueur or Kirsch or rum — some whipped sweetened cream — 2 oz currants — 2 oz raisins — 4 eggs — ½ cup sugar — 1 cup cream — 1 cup milk — 2 oz candied orange peel — 2 oz peeled almonds.

Soften the gelatin in 5 tbsp. cold water. Cut the biscuits in small pieces. Soak them in the Marasquino or Kirsch or rum. Wash the raisins and currants well and cook them for 10 minutes in some water. Drain them. Mix the egg yolks with the sugar. Scald the cream and the milk. Add to the egg yolks and cook in a double boiler until the mixture coats the back of the spoon. Dissolve the gelatin in this mixture. Add currants and raisins and finely chopped orange peel, almonds and liqueur. Stir in this mixture from time to time.

Meanwhile brush a blancmange mold with unbeaten egg white. The leftover egg whites can be used for making a meringue. When the fruit does not sink to the bottom of the mixture any more fill the mold with layers of biscuits and the mixture. But do not start with biscuits or finish with them.

Let the pudding stand in a cool place until quite cold. Unmold it on a glass dish. Garnish the bottom of the pudding with whipped, sweetened cream.

We do not serve a sauce with this pudding. You can serve a vanilla sauce with it if you want.

Cakes and cookies.

Salted cookies
Arnhem girls
Jewish butter cake
Buttercake with almond paste
Limburg pies

Spicy St. Nicholas' doll
Peppernuts
Creamy sugar candies
Snow sponge cake
Christmas ring
Dutch spice cake
Christmas cookies

Salted cookies. (makes 50).
(Zoute bolletjes).

1 cup self-rising flour — ½ cup butter or margarine — salt.

Quickly knead sifted self rising flour, softened butter or margarine and ½ tbsp. salt into a smooth ball. Shape into 50 small balls, ¾″ in diameter. Place on buttered baking-sheet and bake in 350° F. oven for 15 minutes, or until golden yellow (sandcoloured).
"Zoute bolletjes" are mostly served in Holland as an appetizer with the "borrel" (Dutch gin). See also page 104.

Arnhem girls. (Arnhemse meisjes).

1 cup of butter or margarine — ½ cup flour — a pinch of salt — about 4 tbsp. water — 1 egg — sugar for sprinkling.

Make puff pastry in your own manner of the 4 first ingredients. Roll out thinly. Cut out ovals with a cooky cutter of about 2½″. Place on buttered baking-sheet, not too close together. Moisten tops with a mixture of water and beaten egg and sprinkle with sugar. Bake about 10 minutes in a hot oven (450° F.) until done, very crisp and golden brown.

Jewish butter cake. [1]) (Joodse boterkoek).

2 cups flour — 1 cup butter — 1 cup sugar (caster) — 1 small egg, beaten — salt — 3 oz finely chopped candied ginger.

Knead all the ingredients into a smooth paste, keep half the beaten egg for decorating. Butter a pie pan of 1" deep and 8" diameter. Press the dough into it.

Brush the rest of the egg on top. Decorate the top in squares with back of a knife. Bake for 30 minutes in a moderate oven (350° F.) until golden brown. While still hot press the middle of the cake down with the back of a spoon. Cool and when firm to the touch turn out on wire rack.

This cake should be soft inside (but done!) and hard at the outside.

[1]) See note on next page.

88

Butter cake with almond paste. [1])
(Gevulde boterkoek).

For the dough: 2 cups flour — 1 cup butter — 1 cup (caster) sugar — 1 small egg — pinch of salt.

Knead all the ingredients for the dough into a firm ball. Divide the dough in two and press one half into a buttered pie pan of 1″ deep and 8″ diameter. Make the filling.

For the filling: 2 cup blanched almonds — ¼ cup sugar — 1 small egg — grated peel of half a lemon.

Grind the blanched almonds, mix with sugar, beaten egg and lemon peel and grind once more. Place this almond paste on top of the dough layer and press the other half on top of both. Bake in moderate (350° F.) oven until golden brown and done, about one hour. Remove from pan and cool on wire rack. Cut in wedges or diamonds.

[1]) Both these cakes should be made with butter.

89

Limburg pies. (Limburgse vlaaien).

For the dough: a sweet bread dough (or fine bread dough) baked in a 10" round pan or in 4 individual smaller pans, made of 2 cups flour (use your own favourite recipe).

For the filling: any fruit, dried fruit — sugar.

Limburg pies are thin, flat pies made of bread dough. They are made in all sizes from 4 to 20 inches in diameter. For a pie of about 8 inches a dough made of 2 cups flour will suffice. For preparing dough use recipe for sweet bread dough or fine bread dough adding a little butter or margarine. Knead dough, leave it to rise, roll it out thinly, put it in a greased round pan, cover up and leave to rise to double its size.

Prick dough with fork or knife if it has risen too high. Cut e.q. plums into halves, stone them and put them closely together on dough with cut side upwards, or fill pie with stoned cherries or stewed fruit. Bake pie in hot oven (450° F.) for about 30 minutes. Sprinkle fruit with sugar 10 minutes before pie is taken out of oven, sprinkle once more when pie is done. If stewed fruit is used, mix fruit with sugar before filling pie.

St. Nicholas' doll. (Speculaaspop).

3 cups flour — ⅔ cup butter or margarine — ½ cup dark brown sugar[1]) — a pinch each of baking powder and salt — some milk to soften the dough — 1 tsp. cinnamon — ½ tsp. nutmeg — ¼ tsp. powdered cloves — ½ cup almonds, blanched slivered and some halves "for decorating".

Knead all ingredients to a soft ball, except the almonds for decorating. Roll

[1]) When too coarse roll with rolling pin.

out on a floured board to ¼ inch thickness and stamp out shapes with different butterprints or make a "gingerbread doll" or cooky. Bake 25 minutes at 350° F. You can also make them like "Brownies" and cut them into squares (bake longer, 30—35 minutes). You will then call them: "Speculaasjes".

Peppernuts. (Pepernoten).

1¼ cup flour — 1¼ cup self-rising flour — ½ cup brown sugar (see note previous recipe)

— *2 tbsp. water — 1 egg yolk — ¼ tsp. each of cinnamon, nutmeg, powdered cloves — some anise seeds — a pinch of salt.*

Knead all ingredients into a soft ball. Butter two baking sheets. Form about ninety marble-sized balls. Divide them over the sheets, so that they are placed at equal distances from one another. Flatten each ball slightly. Bake about 20 minutes in a moderate oven (350° F.), or until done. (They are then very hard.)
On Dec. 5th "Pepernoten" are often thrown through the slightly opened door by a black-gloved hand, represent-ting "Black Peter", St. Nicholas' faithful helpmate. All the children crawl over the floor on which a white sheet is spread and grab what they can, while singing one of the popular St. Nicholas songs. A loud doorbell ringing just before this procedure enhances the excitement.

Snow sponge cake.

(Moskovische tulband).

For a fluted pudding mold of 8" dia-meter and one small round fluted tea-cake tin.

4 eggs — ⅓ cup sugar — vanilla essence or grated lemon peel — 1 cup flour (sifted) — ⅓ cup hard butter or margarine — confectioner's sugar.

Butter the big and the small mold. Coat with sifted confectioner's sugar. Separate the eggs. Add sugar and lemon rind to the egg yolks and beat them with a wooden spoon until of a creamy consistency (takes about 20 minutes). Cut the butter into the flour in very small pieces. Then whip the whites until stiff. Put the egg yolks, the flour mixture and the salt on top of the whites. *Do not stir anymore.*

Fold the ingredients into the whites with a metal spoon until all the flour has been taken up. Then immediately fill the molds for ⅔ and bake the cake for 20 minutes in a moderate oven (350° F.). Remove the small cake as soon as it is done. Take the snow cake out of the oven. Let it stand for 5 minutes. Then turn it out on a wire rack. Leave to cool. When cold, put the little cake on top of the big one and dust with a thick layer of sifted confectioner's sugar.

This cake can be decorated for Christmas, with a sprig of holly and a red ribbon and for Easter with an Easter-chicken.

The Dutch serve it also as a traditional cake on New Year's Day with morning-coffee.

Christmas ring. (Kerstkrans).

Puff-pastry: 1 cup flour — ½ cup butter or margarine — water to mix — salt.

For the filling: almond paste: ¾ cup shelled, blanched and peeled almonds — ¼ cup granulated sugar — 1 egg — the peel of 1 lemon — 5 candied cherries.

To decorate: thin lemon icing — apricot preserve — candied cherries, red and green — candied orange peel — candied lemon peel or angelica — a red ribbon — holly.

Make the filling at least one month in advance. Store in jar. Grind the almonds very finely, add the sugar and the egg, also the grated peel. Mix well. Grind again. Store. When necessary knead through and add some water if paste is too stiff. Make the puff-pastry your favorite way. Roll out into a long strip of $\frac{1}{8}''$ thick, 4" wide. Brush your baking-sheet with water. Take a pancover that will nearly fit the baking-sheet. Put it in the middle and trace the circumference, this will guide you when forming the ring. Shape almond paste into a roll of nearly the same length. Press 10 halved candied cherries at equal intervals into the almond paste roll. They must not be visible anymore. Now place the almond roll on the dough, a little above the centre. Wet the lower part of the dough with water and wrap it loosely around the almond paste roll. Put it on the baking-sheet: the "ring" will guide you. Seal the join well and turn roll until the join faces down. Form a ring by joining the two ends together with some water. Brush with beaten egg. Allow to stand for 15 minutes in a cool place. Then bake for 20 minutes in a hot oven (450° F.) until golden brown. When done, coat the ring thinly with preserve and when still *hot*, coat with thin icing (with a few drops of lemon juice). Cool. When firm, take from sheet and cool on wire rack. Decorate with halved candied cherries, orange peel and lemon peel cut in leaf shapes. Tie a ribbon round the ring where the two ends meet and decorate with holly.

Dutch spice cake. (Ontbijtkoek).

2 cups self rising flour — ½ cup dark brown sugar (demerara sugar) — ⅓ cup molasses or treacle — 1 cup milk — 1 tsp. each ground cloves, cinnamon and ginger — ½ tsp. grated nutmeg — pinch of salt.

Combine all the ingredients to a smooth paste. Butter an oblong 8″ × 3″ cake tin, fill with dough and bake for about one hour in a slow oven (300° F.). When cooked, allow to cool and keep in a tin or in the bread-bin for 24 hours before serving. This cake keeps moist when put in the bread-bin with the bread. The Dutch serve it with their "elevenses", buttered or on a slice of bread for breakfast.

Christmas cookies. (Kerstkransjes).

2 cups flour — ⅔ cup butter or margarine — ¾ cup sugar — 1 tbsp. milk — 1 tsp. baking powder — grated peel of ½ lemon — salt — 1 egg — rock sugar and ¼ cup shelled almonds.

Knead flour, butter, sugar, milk, baking powder, lemon peel and salt into a soft ball and leave to stand for one hour.

Roll out sections of the dough on a floured board to ⅛ inch thickness and cut out circles with a 2½ inch tumbler. Place the cookies on a buttered bakingsheet, then cut out the centre with a small round object such as a thimble. Remove these centres and use them to make more cookies.

Coat dough "wreaths" with beaten egg and sprinkle them with a mixture of rock sugar and blanched, chopped almonds. Bake about 15—20 minutes in a 350° F. oven until golden brown. Leave to cool on sheet until no longer soft. Remove

and cool further on a wire rack.
Pass gaily-coloured ribbons through the holes and hang them on the Christmas tree.

Miscellaneous.

Fried rice.

Creamy sugar candies.

"Kandeel" (a beverage).

"Slemp" (a beverage).

Savory appetizers.

Fried rice. (Nasi goreng).

This dish originated in the Dutch East Indies (now Indonesia) and is very much liked by the Dutch. It is eaten out of a soup plate with a large spoon.

Butter, margarine or oil — 3 tbsp. very finely chopped onions — some garlic or garlic powder — spices: ½ tsp. coriander, ½ tsp. caraway seed — ½ tsp. finely chopped chili (hot red pepper) — 1 cup chopped ham or cooked pork — salt — pepper — 3½ cup cold cooked rice — an omelet, made of 3 eggs —if desired 1 cup cut-up shrimps — cucumber salad.

Fry the onions in the butter until light brown. Add the garlic, the spices and the meat. Season with salt and pepper. Fry the meat for a few minutes. Add the very fluffy and dry rice. Keep stirring until the rice browns lightly. If too dry add some meat stock. Add the shrimps if desired.
Now bake an omelet, cut in thin slices. Put the rice-mixture in a shallow dish and garnish with the omelet slices.
This dish may be served with cucumber salad. And one should drink a glass of beer with it. If you want it rather "hot"

add some chili powder or very little dried chili.

When available in your neighbourhood serve with "prawn chips" (kroepoek) made of dried shrimps fried in oil. You might be able to get it in a shop where they sell produce from Singapore or Indonesia.

Creamy Sugar Candies.
(Roomborstplaat).

1½ cups white sugar — 1 cup brown sugar — ½ cup light cream — 1¼ tbsp. butter and some butter for brushing the molds — 3 tbsp. fruit-flavored extract or 4 tbsp. instant coffee or 2 tbsp. cocoa.

Place tin rings or other open molds on a large piece of wax paper. (Lids of tins may substitute them). Brush paper and molds with softened butter. Put sugar, cream, butter and the coffee or cocoa flavoring in a saucepan (if fruit extract is used, it should be added later). Bring slowly to the boil without stirring, until a syrup results; this takes about five minutes. A drop of this syrup dropped into a cup of cold water should form a little ball or pea, or if syrup spins a thread.

Remove pan from heat at once (stir in fruit extract). Stir to cool and pour into the prepared molds when the syrup can hardly be poured any more, to a thickness of about $\frac{1}{4}$ to $\frac{1}{2}$ inch; the smaller the molds, the thinner the "borstplaat". Cool in the molds, then remove.

Beverages. (Dranken).

There are a few typical beverages we make for special occasions. A traditional drink, we offer to our visitors when a baby is born is "Kandeel". It is served in small cups and poured out of a pitcher (jug). In the pitcher a long stick of cinnamon is stuck. And a bow is tied round it; a pink one for a girl, a blue one for a boy.

Kandeel. (for 6 cups).

½ cup water — 20 cloves — a cinnamon stick — grated peel of ½ lemon — 6 egg yolks — ½ bottle of Rhine wine — 1 cup sugar.

Tie the spices in a piece of cloth. Hang it in the water and simmer for 1 hour (add some water when it evaporates). Cool. Beat the egg yolks with sugar until creamy. Add wine and liquid. Put in double boiler and stir until it thickens.
Another beverage the Hollanders drink after skating is:

Slemp

spices: ½ tsp. tea, cinnamon stick of 1", saffron, 2 cloves, mace — 4 cups milk — grated peel of ½ lemon — 2 tbsp. sugar — salt.

Put the spices in a piece of cloth. Tie with a string. Boil the milk. Hang the spices in the milk (tie the string to the handle of the pan). Add lemon and salt and simmer for one hour. Then remove spice-bag. Add sugar and serve piping hot.

Savory appetizers. (Bitterballen).
Amount: 25.

1 cup thick white sauce — 2 cups chopped cooked meat (roastbeef or veal or ham or a mixture of all three) — 1 tbsp. minced parsley — pepper — salt — Worcestershire sauce — 1 egg — fine dry bread crumbs — cooking-oil — wooden picks — mustard.

Mix sauce, meat, parsley. Add pepper, salt and sauce to taste. Chill. Shape into balls (1 inch). Roll in bread crumbs. Dry for two hours. Mix egg with 2 tbsp. water. Dip balls in egg, again in bread crumbs. Fry in hot deep fat (400° F) for 1 to 2 minutes. Drain. Serve piping hot, on a wooden pick. Mustard can be handed round or put on a small dish.

The word "bitter" comes from "gin and bitter" and does not mean the opposite of "sweet".

The people in the Netherlands serve these, when drinking their "Dutch gin", before dinner, called "Borrel". But always serve "jenever" (Dutch gin) iced! Not "with ice"!

Index (English).

Index (Hollands).